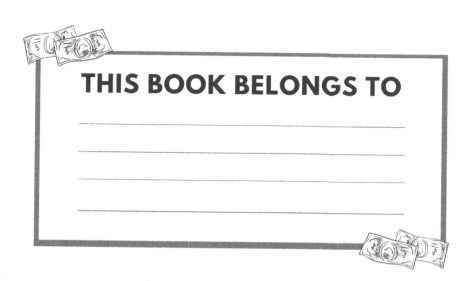

THIS BOOK BELONGS TO

_____

_____

_____

_____

D1607755

SIMPLE BUDGET LISTS

Budget by paycheck or by month with this dual purpose budgeting planner. Do what works best for your personal finances and situation.

BUDGET PLANNER

MONTH / PAY PERIOD _____

list all income sources by month or paycheck - total at bottom.

list any notes, goals, paycheck dates, amounts, key reminders & more.

list savings plan and/or sinking funds for future irregular expenses; use additional savings tracker for more detail.

list all variable expenses like groceries, eating out, clothing, gas, personal care, etc. - amounts may vary each month and cash envelopes are recommended.

list extra payments toward debts to keep track of payoffs; use additional debt tracker for more detail.

list all fixed expenses like housing, car, insurance, utilities, memberships, etc. - most have due dates and autopay is recommended.

list difference between income, savings, fixed bills, variable expenses, and debt - ideally total should be ZERO or in the positive.

INCOME	BUDGET	ACTUAL

NOTES / GOALS

SAVING / GIVING	BUDGET	ACTUAL
TOTAL:		

EXPENSES / VAR.	BUDGET	ACTUAL
TOTAL:		

DUE	BILLS / FIXED	BUDGET	ACTUAL
	TOTAL:		

DEBT / PAYMENTS	BUDGET	ACTUAL
TOTAL:		

OVERALL	BUDGET	ACTUAL
TOTAL INCOME		
TOTAL SAVINGS		
TOTAL BILLS		
TOTAL EXPENSES		
TOTAL DEBT		
= DIFFERENCE		

Do not save what is left after spending; instead spend what is left after saving."
-WARREN BUFFET-

BUDGET PLANNER

MONTH / PAY PERIOD: _____

INCOME	BUDGET	ACTUAL

NOTES / GOALS:

SAVING / GIVING	BUDGET	ACTUAL
TOTAL:		

EXPENSES / VAR.	BUDGET	ACTUAL
TOTAL:		

DUE	BILLS / FIXED	BUDGET	ACTUAL
	TOTAL:		

DEBT / PAYMENTS	BUDGET	ACTUAL
TOTAL:		

OVERALL	BUDGET	ACTUAL
TOTAL INCOME		
TOTAL SAVINGS		
TOTAL BILLS		
TOTAL EXPENSES		
TOTAL DEBT		
= DIFFERENCE		

BUDGET PLANNER

MONTH / PAY PERIOD: _____

INCOME	BUDGET	ACTUAL

NOTES / GOALS:

SAVING / GIVING	BUDGET	ACTUAL
TOTAL:		

EXPENSES / VAR.	BUDGET	ACTUAL
TOTAL:		

DUE	BILLS / FIXED	BUDGET	ACTUAL
	TOTAL:		

DEBT / PAYMENTS	BUDGET	ACTUAL
TOTAL:		

OVERALL	BUDGET	ACTUAL
TOTAL INCOME		
TOTAL SAVINGS		
TOTAL BILLS		
TOTAL EXPENSES		
TOTAL DEBT		
= DIFFERENCE		

BUDGET PLANNER

MONTH / PAY PERIOD: _____

INCOME	BUDGET	ACTUAL

NOTES / GOALS:

SAVING / GIVING	BUDGET	ACTUAL
TOTAL:		

EXPENSES / VAR.	BUDGET	ACTUAL
TOTAL:		

DUE	BILLS / FIXED	BUDGET	ACTUAL
	TOTAL:		

DEBT / PAYMENTS	BUDGET	ACTUAL
TOTAL:		

OVERALL	BUDGET	ACTUAL
TOTAL INCOME		
TOTAL SAVINGS		
TOTAL BILLS		
TOTAL EXPENSES		
TOTAL DEBT		
= DIFFERENCE		

BUDGET PLANNER

MONTH / PAY PERIOD: _____

INCOME	BUDGET	ACTUAL

NOTES / GOALS:

SAVING / GIVING	BUDGET	ACTUAL
TOTAL:		

EXPENSES / VAR.	BUDGET	ACTUAL
TOTAL:		

DUE	BILLS / FIXED	BUDGET	ACTUAL
	TOTAL:		

DEBT / PAYMENTS	BUDGET	ACTUAL
TOTAL:		

OVERALL	BUDGET	ACTUAL
TOTAL INCOME		
TOTAL SAVINGS		
TOTAL BILLS		
TOTAL EXPENSES		
TOTAL DEBT		
= DIFFERENCE		

BUDGET PLANNER

MONTH / PAY PERIOD: _____

INCOME	BUDGET	ACTUAL

NOTES / GOALS:

SAVING / GIVING	BUDGET	ACTUAL
TOTAL:		

EXPENSES / VAR.	BUDGET	ACTUAL
TOTAL:		

DUE	BILLS / FIXED	BUDGET	ACTUAL
	TOTAL:		

DEBT / PAYMENTS	BUDGET	ACTUAL
TOTAL:		

OVERALL	BUDGET	ACTUAL
TOTAL INCOME		
TOTAL SAVINGS		
TOTAL BILLS		
TOTAL EXPENSES		
TOTAL DEBT		
= DIFFERENCE		

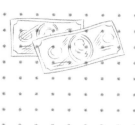

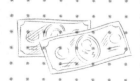

BUDGET PLANNER

MONTH / PAY PERIOD: _____

INCOME	BUDGET	ACTUAL

NOTES / GOALS:

SAVING / GIVING	BUDGET	ACTUAL
TOTAL:		

EXPENSES / VAR.	BUDGET	ACTUAL
TOTAL:		

DUE	BILLS / FIXED	BUDGET	ACTUAL
	TOTAL:		

DEBT / PAYMENTS	BUDGET	ACTUAL
TOTAL:		

OVERALL	BUDGET	ACTUAL
TOTAL INCOME		
TOTAL SAVINGS		
TOTAL BILLS		
TOTAL EXPENSES		
TOTAL DEBT		
= DIFFERENCE		

BUDGET PLANNER

MONTH / PAY PERIOD: _____

INCOME	BUDGET	ACTUAL

NOTES / GOALS:

SAVING / GIVING	BUDGET	ACTUAL
TOTAL:		

EXPENSES / VAR.	BUDGET	ACTUAL
TOTAL:		

DUE	BILLS / FIXED	BUDGET	ACTUAL
	TOTAL:		

DEBT / PAYMENTS	BUDGET	ACTUAL
TOTAL:		

OVERALL	BUDGET	ACTUAL
TOTAL INCOME		
TOTAL SAVINGS		
TOTAL BILLS		
TOTAL EXPENSES		
TOTAL DEBT		
= DIFFERENCE		

BUDGET PLANNER

MONTH / PAY PERIOD: _____

INCOME	BUDGET	ACTUAL

NOTES / GOALS:

SAVING / GIVING	BUDGET	ACTUAL
TOTAL:		

EXPENSES / VAR.	BUDGET	ACTUAL
TOTAL:		

DUE	BILLS / FIXED	BUDGET	ACTUAL
	TOTAL:		

DEBT / PAYMENTS	BUDGET	ACTUAL
TOTAL:		

OVERALL	BUDGET	ACTUAL
TOTAL INCOME		
TOTAL SAVINGS		
TOTAL BILLS		
TOTAL EXPENSES		
TOTAL DEBT		
= DIFFERENCE		

BUDGET PLANNER

MONTH / PAY PERIOD: _____

INCOME	BUDGET	ACTUAL

NOTES / GOALS:

SAVING / GIVING	BUDGET	ACTUAL
TOTAL:		

DUE	BILLS / FIXED	BUDGET	ACTUAL
	TOTAL:		

EXPENSES / VAR.	BUDGET	ACTUAL
TOTAL:		

DEBT / PAYMENTS	BUDGET	ACTUAL
TOTAL:		

OVERALL	BUDGET	ACTUAL
TOTAL INCOME		
TOTAL SAVINGS		
TOTAL BILLS		
TOTAL EXPENSES		
TOTAL DEBT		
= DIFFERENCE		

BUDGET PLANNER

MONTH / PAY PERIOD: _____

INCOME	BUDGET	ACTUAL

NOTES / GOALS:

SAVING / GIVING	BUDGET	ACTUAL
TOTAL:		

EXPENSES / VAR.	BUDGET	ACTUAL
TOTAL:		

DUE	BILLS / FIXED	BUDGET	ACTUAL
	TOTAL:		

DEBT / PAYMENTS	BUDGET	ACTUAL
TOTAL:		

OVERALL	BUDGET	ACTUAL
TOTAL INCOME		
TOTAL SAVINGS		
TOTAL BILLS		
TOTAL EXPENSES		
TOTAL DEBT		
= DIFFERENCE		

BUDGET PLANNER

MONTH / PAY PERIOD: _____

INCOME	BUDGET	ACTUAL

NOTES / GOALS:

SAVING / GIVING	BUDGET	ACTUAL
TOTAL:		

EXPENSES / VAR.	BUDGET	ACTUAL
TOTAL:		

DUE	BILLS / FIXED	BUDGET	ACTUAL
	TOTAL:		

DEBT / PAYMENTS	BUDGET	ACTUAL
TOTAL:		

OVERALL	BUDGET	ACTUAL
TOTAL INCOME		
TOTAL SAVINGS		
TOTAL BILLS		
TOTAL EXPENSES		
TOTAL DEBT		
= DIFFERENCE		

BUDGET PLANNER

MONTH / PAY PERIOD: _____

INCOME	BUDGET	ACTUAL

NOTES / GOALS:

SAVING / GIVING	BUDGET	ACTUAL
TOTAL:		

DUE	BILLS / FIXED	BUDGET	ACTUAL
	TOTAL:		

EXPENSES / VAR.	BUDGET	ACTUAL
TOTAL:		

DEBT / PAYMENTS	BUDGET	ACTUAL
TOTAL:		

OVERALL	BUDGET	ACTUAL
TOTAL INCOME		
TOTAL SAVINGS		
TOTAL BILLS		
TOTAL EXPENSES		
TOTAL DEBT		
= DIFFERENCE		

BUDGET PLANNER

MONTH / PAY PERIOD: _____

INCOME	BUDGET	ACTUAL

NOTES / GOALS:

SAVING / GIVING	BUDGET	ACTUAL
TOTAL:		

DUE	BILLS / FIXED	BUDGET	ACTUAL
	TOTAL:		

EXPENSES / VAR.	BUDGET	ACTUAL
TOTAL:		

DEBT / PAYMENTS	BUDGET	ACTUAL
TOTAL:		

OVERALL	BUDGET	ACTUAL
TOTAL INCOME		
TOTAL SAVINGS		
TOTAL BILLS		
TOTAL EXPENSES		
TOTAL DEBT		
= DIFFERENCE		

BUDGET PLANNER

MONTH / PAY PERIOD: _____

INCOME	BUDGET	ACTUAL

NOTES / GOALS:

SAVING / GIVING	BUDGET	ACTUAL
TOTAL:		

EXPENSES / VAR.	BUDGET	ACTUAL
TOTAL:		

DUE	BILLS / FIXED	BUDGET	ACTUAL
	TOTAL:		

DEBT / PAYMENTS	BUDGET	ACTUAL
TOTAL:		

OVERALL	BUDGET	ACTUAL
TOTAL INCOME		
TOTAL SAVINGS		
TOTAL BILLS		
TOTAL EXPENSES		
TOTAL DEBT		
= DIFFERENCE		

BUDGET PLANNER

MONTH / PAY PERIOD: _____

INCOME	BUDGET	ACTUAL

NOTES / GOALS:

SAVING / GIVING	BUDGET	ACTUAL
TOTAL:		

DUE	BILLS / FIXED	BUDGET	ACTUAL
	TOTAL:		

EXPENSES / VAR.	BUDGET	ACTUAL
TOTAL:		

DEBT / PAYMENTS	BUDGET	ACTUAL
TOTAL:		

OVERALL	BUDGET	ACTUAL
TOTAL INCOME		
TOTAL SAVINGS		
TOTAL BILLS		
TOTAL EXPENSES		
TOTAL DEBT		
= DIFFERENCE		

BUDGET PLANNER

MONTH / PAY PERIOD: _____

INCOME	BUDGET	ACTUAL

NOTES / GOALS:

SAVING / GIVING	BUDGET	ACTUAL
TOTAL:		

EXPENSES / VAR.	BUDGET	ACTUAL
TOTAL:		

DUE	BILLS / FIXED	BUDGET	ACTUAL
	TOTAL:		

DEBT / PAYMENTS	BUDGET	ACTUAL
TOTAL:		

OVERALL	BUDGET	ACTUAL
TOTAL INCOME		
TOTAL SAVINGS		
TOTAL BILLS		
TOTAL EXPENSES		
TOTAL DEBT		
= DIFFERENCE		

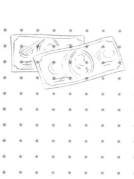

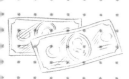

BUDGET PLANNER

MONTH / PAY PERIOD: _____

INCOME	BUDGET	ACTUAL

NOTES / GOALS:

SAVING / GIVING	BUDGET	ACTUAL
TOTAL:		

EXPENSES / VAR.	BUDGET	ACTUAL
TOTAL:		

DUE	BILLS / FIXED	BUDGET	ACTUAL
	TOTAL:		

DEBT / PAYMENTS	BUDGET	ACTUAL
TOTAL:		

OVERALL	BUDGET	ACTUAL
TOTAL INCOME		
TOTAL SAVINGS		
TOTAL BILLS		
TOTAL EXPENSES		
TOTAL DEBT		
= DIFFERENCE		

BUDGET PLANNER

MONTH / PAY PERIOD: _____

INCOME	BUDGET	ACTUAL

NOTES / GOALS:

SAVING / GIVING	BUDGET	ACTUAL
TOTAL:		

EXPENSES / VAR.	BUDGET	ACTUAL
TOTAL:		

DUE	BILLS / FIXED	BUDGET	ACTUAL
	TOTAL:		

DEBT / PAYMENTS	BUDGET	ACTUAL
TOTAL:		

OVERALL	BUDGET	ACTUAL
TOTAL INCOME		
TOTAL SAVINGS		
TOTAL BILLS		
TOTAL EXPENSES		
TOTAL DEBT		
= DIFFERENCE		

BUDGET PLANNER

MONTH / PAY PERIOD: _____

INCOME	BUDGET	ACTUAL

NOTES / GOALS:

SAVING / GIVING	BUDGET	ACTUAL
TOTAL:		

EXPENSES / VAR.	BUDGET	ACTUAL
TOTAL:		

DUE	BILLS / FIXED	BUDGET	ACTUAL
	TOTAL:		

DEBT / PAYMENTS	BUDGET	ACTUAL
TOTAL:		

OVERALL	BUDGET	ACTUAL
TOTAL INCOME		
TOTAL SAVINGS		
TOTAL BILLS		
TOTAL EXPENSES		
TOTAL DEBT		
= DIFFERENCE		

BUDGET PLANNER

MONTH / PAY PERIOD: _____

INCOME	BUDGET	ACTUAL

NOTES / GOALS:

SAVING / GIVING	BUDGET	ACTUAL
TOTAL:		

EXPENSES / VAR.	BUDGET	ACTUAL
TOTAL:		

DUE	BILLS / FIXED	BUDGET	ACTUAL
	TOTAL:		

DEBT / PAYMENTS	BUDGET	ACTUAL
TOTAL:		

OVERALL	BUDGET	ACTUAL
TOTAL INCOME		
TOTAL SAVINGS		
TOTAL BILLS		
TOTAL EXPENSES		
TOTAL DEBT		
= DIFFERENCE		

BUDGET PLANNER

MONTH / PAY PERIOD: _____

INCOME	BUDGET	ACTUAL

SAVING / GIVING	BUDGET	ACTUAL
TOTAL:		

EXPENSES / VAR.	BUDGET	ACTUAL
TOTAL:		

DUE	BILLS / FIXED	BUDGET	ACTUAL
	TOTAL:		

DEBT / PAYMENTS	BUDGET	ACTUAL
TOTAL:		

OVERALL	BUDGET	ACTUAL
TOTAL INCOME		
TOTAL SAVINGS		
TOTAL BILLS		
TOTAL EXPENSES		
TOTAL DEBT		
= DIFFERENCE		

BUDGET PLANNER

MONTH / PAY PERIOD: _____

INCOME	BUDGET	ACTUAL

NOTES / GOALS:

SAVING / GIVING	BUDGET	ACTUAL
TOTAL:		

EXPENSES / VAR.	BUDGET	ACTUAL
TOTAL:		

DUE	BILLS / FIXED	BUDGET	ACTUAL
	TOTAL:		

DEBT / PAYMENTS	BUDGET	ACTUAL
TOTAL:		

OVERALL	BUDGET	ACTUAL
TOTAL INCOME		
TOTAL SAVINGS		
TOTAL BILLS		
TOTAL EXPENSES		
TOTAL DEBT		
= DIFFERENCE		

BUDGET PLANNER

MONTH / PAY PERIOD: _____

INCOME	BUDGET	ACTUAL

NOTES / GOALS:

SAVING / GIVING	BUDGET	ACTUAL
TOTAL:		

DUE	BILLS / FIXED	BUDGET	ACTUAL
	TOTAL:		

EXPENSES / VAR.	BUDGET	ACTUAL
TOTAL:		

DEBT / PAYMENTS	BUDGET	ACTUAL
TOTAL:		

OVERALL	BUDGET	ACTUAL
TOTAL INCOME		
TOTAL SAVINGS		
TOTAL BILLS		
TOTAL EXPENSES		
TOTAL DEBT		
= DIFFERENCE		

BUDGET PLANNER

MONTH / PAY PERIOD: _____

INCOME	BUDGET	ACTUAL

NOTES / GOALS:

SAVING / GIVING	BUDGET	ACTUAL
TOTAL:		

DUE	BILLS / FIXED	BUDGET	ACTUAL
	TOTAL:		

EXPENSES / VAR.	BUDGET	ACTUAL
TOTAL:		

DEBT / PAYMENTS	BUDGET	ACTUAL
TOTAL:		

OVERALL	BUDGET	ACTUAL
TOTAL INCOME		
TOTAL SAVINGS		
TOTAL BILLS		
TOTAL EXPENSES		
TOTAL DEBT		
= DIFFERENCE		

BUDGET PLANNER

MONTH / PAY PERIOD: _____

INCOME	BUDGET	ACTUAL

NOTES / GOALS:

SAVING / GIVING	BUDGET	ACTUAL
TOTAL:		

EXPENSES / VAR.	BUDGET	ACTUAL
TOTAL:		

DUE	BILLS / FIXED	BUDGET	ACTUAL
	TOTAL:		

DEBT / PAYMENTS	BUDGET	ACTUAL
TOTAL:		

OVERALL	BUDGET	ACTUAL
TOTAL INCOME		
TOTAL SAVINGS		
TOTAL BILLS		
TOTAL EXPENSES		
TOTAL DEBT		
= DIFFERENCE		

BUDGET PLANNER

MONTH / PAY PERIOD: _____

INCOME	BUDGET	ACTUAL

NOTES / GOALS:

SAVING / GIVING	BUDGET	ACTUAL
TOTAL:		

EXPENSES / VAR.	BUDGET	ACTUAL
TOTAL:		

DUE	BILLS / FIXED	BUDGET	ACTUAL
	TOTAL:		

DEBT / PAYMENTS	BUDGET	ACTUAL
TOTAL:		

OVERALL	BUDGET	ACTUAL
TOTAL INCOME		
TOTAL SAVINGS		
TOTAL BILLS		
TOTAL EXPENSES		
TOTAL DEBT		
= DIFFERENCE		

BUDGET PLANNER

MONTH / PAY PERIOD: _____

INCOME	BUDGET	ACTUAL

NOTES / GOALS:

SAVING / GIVING	BUDGET	ACTUAL
TOTAL:		

DUE	BILLS / FIXED	BUDGET	ACTUAL
	TOTAL:		

EXPENSES / VAR.	BUDGET	ACTUAL
	TOTAL:	

DEBT / PAYMENTS	BUDGET	ACTUAL
TOTAL:		

OVERALL	BUDGET	ACTUAL
TOTAL INCOME		
TOTAL SAVINGS		
TOTAL BILLS		
TOTAL EXPENSES		
TOTAL DEBT		
= DIFFERENCE		

BUDGET PLANNER

MONTH / PAY PERIOD: _____

INCOME	BUDGET	ACTUAL

NOTES / GOALS:

SAVING / GIVING	BUDGET	ACTUAL
TOTAL:		

EXPENSES / VAR.	BUDGET	ACTUAL
TOTAL:		

DUE	BILLS / FIXED	BUDGET	ACTUAL
	TOTAL:		

DEBT / PAYMENTS	BUDGET	ACTUAL
TOTAL:		

OVERALL	BUDGET	ACTUAL
TOTAL INCOME		
TOTAL SAVINGS		
TOTAL BILLS		
TOTAL EXPENSES		
TOTAL DEBT		
= DIFFERENCE		

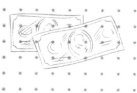

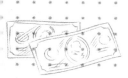

BUDGET PLANNER

MONTH / PAY PERIOD: _____

INCOME	BUDGET	ACTUAL

NOTES / GOALS:

SAVING / GIVING	BUDGET	ACTUAL
TOTAL:		

EXPENSES / VAR.	BUDGET	ACTUAL
TOTAL:		

DUE	BILLS / FIXED	BUDGET	ACTUAL
	TOTAL:		

DEBT / PAYMENTS	BUDGET	ACTUAL
TOTAL:		

OVERALL	BUDGET	ACTUAL
TOTAL INCOME		
TOTAL SAVINGS		
TOTAL BILLS		
TOTAL EXPENSES		
TOTAL DEBT		
= DIFFERENCE		

BUDGET PLANNER

MONTH / PAY PERIOD: _____

INCOME	BUDGET	ACTUAL

NOTES / GOALS:

SAVING / GIVING	BUDGET	ACTUAL
TOTAL:		

EXPENSES / VAR.	BUDGET	ACTUAL
TOTAL:		

DUE	BILLS / FIXED	BUDGET	ACTUAL
	TOTAL:		

DEBT / PAYMENTS	BUDGET	ACTUAL
TOTAL:		

OVERALL	BUDGET	ACTUAL
TOTAL INCOME		
TOTAL SAVINGS		
TOTAL BILLS		
TOTAL EXPENSES		
TOTAL DEBT		
= DIFFERENCE		

BUDGET PLANNER

MONTH / PAY PERIOD: _____

INCOME	BUDGET	ACTUAL

NOTES / GOALS:

SAVING / GIVING	BUDGET	ACTUAL
TOTAL:		

EXPENSES / VAR.	BUDGET	ACTUAL
TOTAL:		

DUE	BILLS / FIXED	BUDGET	ACTUAL
	TOTAL:		

DEBT / PAYMENTS	BUDGET	ACTUAL
TOTAL:		

OVERALL	BUDGET	ACTUAL
TOTAL INCOME		
TOTAL SAVINGS		
TOTAL BILLS		
TOTAL EXPENSES		
TOTAL DEBT		
= DIFFERENCE		

Made in United States
North Haven, CT
28 June 2022

20699663R00075